REFORMED!

A story of Jenny Geddes

by

Helen Welsh

rooshie doo

Published by Gallus Publications,
PO Box 29055,
Dunfermline KY11 4YL

Cover design by Liam Doherty, with original artwork by Darren Brown of Commercial Primary School, Dunfermline (front cover) and Megan McAuley of St. Paul's Primary School, Glenrothes (back cover). Illustrations by Frank McCormick.

ISBN 0-9546625-0-4

A catalogue record for this book is available from the British Library.

Printed and bound by Printing Services (Scotland) Ltd., Broomhead Drive, Dunfermline.

Author's acknowledgements

I am grateful to David Campbell and Linda Brownlie for their advice on matters ecclesiastical and obstetric, respectively. Also to Gordon Donaldson, former Principal of Edinburgh Theological College, for his text 'The Scottish Dimension: the story of Christianity in Scotland, with particular reference to the Episcopal Church'. Also to the lady guide in St. Giles Cathedral who reminded me why we need to drop our denominational defences.

Helen Welsh, Dunfermline July 2004

EDINBURGH.

CHAPTER ONE

King Charles himself couldn't have hoped for a finer night to celebrate his coronation. The day had been hot and overcast, making everyone bad-tempered and headachey and sullen. The clouds, sitting low over Edinburgh's skyline, were thick and grey and heavy. Then suddenly about mid-afternoon came the first rumble of thunder, the first bright flash of lightning. And the first raindrops began to fall.

People thought it must be an omen. But was it a good or a bad omen?

'Thunder and lightning! God is cursing the new king! We shouldn't have brought back the monarchy after all!'

'Havers! The thunder and lightning are God's way of marking the occasion! The rain will help the barley grow - we'll have a good harvest! This is a sign of better things to come!'

'The last one had his head chopped off! Maybe we should chop this one's head off too!'

'Dinna be daft. Gie the man a chance.'

And while they argued, the rain fell, the sky cleared,

1

the sun came out, and before teatime the weather had settled down into a glorious, warm, fresh, summer's evening.

And as everyone agreed, what better evening for the big street party to celebrate the return of the monarchy to Scotland – and England – after eleven years in the wilderness.

Life had been very strict and plain in the past eleven years, when there was no king on the throne. Fun was seen as frivolous. Laughter was seen as disrespectful. Everything was grim. The people were desperate for a right good party. So, tonight was the night; there was plenty more sun in the sky to dry the rain off the streets before nightfall; and there would be no clouds to obscure the fine full moon which would light up the streets for the revellers.

The dates for big occasions were always set in accordance with the full moon – how else would people be able to find their way round in the dark? So Edinburgh was well lit up that night, all the way from the castle, down the royal mile to Holyrood House, down in the Grassmarket and the Cowgate, over by the Nor Loch, which lay in the lee of the castle. Those who had fretted about the thunder and lightning relaxed and agreed that yes indeed, this was a fine night for coronation celebrations; and God must be very pleased with them for bringing this occasion about. Why else would he have graced the occasion with such fine weather? God must like kings and queens and all that went with them. A fine night it would be.

CHAPTER TWO

It was a feast for the eyes, the ears, the nose, the belly. Down in the Grassmarket the innkeepers had set out their tables and chairs in the street. Crowds thronged up and down, jolly and good-natured; the night was young, there was a bit of spare cash due to the good harvest, and there was every reason to hope for a night to remember.

At one end of the Grassmarket, deep below the castle walls, an enterprising butcher had built a bonfire deep in a pit, and set up a massive spit over it. Just the day before, he had slaughtered a hog, led in on a string by a farmer out in Silverknowes. It was the best hog the butcher had seen for years, with its long, firm, bristly back and its fine fat thighs. The farmer had haggled hard, and the butcher had been forced to pay a whole guinea more than he had intended; but hopefully the investment would pay off. Tonight, he expected to make a handsome profit.

First thing this morning, the hog had been hoisted on the spit and set to roast. By now, its skin was golden and crisp, its flesh succulent, and the smell completely tantalising. For a penny, a hungry peasant could buy a hunk of bread and a thick slice of fragrant, steaming roast pork with its crispy golden crackling. Packs of dogs hovered at a safe distance, their hungry eyes targeted on the hog.

Occasionally someone threw a bone, and piles of mongrels would tumble over each other, snapping and biting for a share of the bounty. This was better sport than chasing rats.

Dotted along the street were peddlers tending smaller fires, over which chestnuts roasted, their skins bursting to reveal the sweet white flesh within. Others baked whole apples in the embers. The perfumes were rich and sweet, and people's mouths watered in anticipation.

Most people wandered up and down the street, eating pork and chestnuts and apples and drinking ale. It was a fine night for a wander. The gentry had seats, set

out at long trestle tables in front of the inns. Servant children waited on them, their bare feet scampering over the cobbles, in and out of the cellars. It was hot, hard work but there was such excitement in the air, and the likelihood of good tips; no-one minded being a servant that night. It was a good chance to earn a few extra pennies to take home to mother.

It took two servants to hoist out, between them, the long wooden platters laden with all sorts of delicacies: hard-boiled pigeons' eggs; herrings in vinegar; sheep's cheeses; apples; walnuts. That was just a wee starter, to whet the gentlemen's appetites. Then the servants had to clear away anything that remained (and try to wolf down the leftovers when nobody was looking). Then refill the gentlemen's tankards, then back to the kitchen to collect yet another platter, much longer and heavier than the first. On this, there reposed roast beef, glistening on its ribs; great haunches of venison; deep ashets of pigs' kidneys; and a huge misshapen bird that turned out to be a pigeon stuffed with raisins, tucked inside a de-boned chicken, tucked inside a de-boned goose. Nellie, the carving-woman, cut it expertly, so that you could see in one slice the different meats that had been cooked together – a morsel of pigeon surrounded by chicken then goose, light meat against dark. Golden grease dripped down the gentlemen's beards, and up Nellie's arms to her elbows. The whole feast was magnificent. Especially after all the long dull years of porridge and kale.

Two fiddlers set up under a tree and tuned up their instruments, the first scratch and twang bringing clusters of beggar children running to see what was happening. Soon the musicians were fiddling away merrily, reels and jigs spilling out into the night. First the children, then groups of adults started to tap their feet. Then here and there they began to take each others' arms; and the dancing began. The dancers shouted out requests for their favourite tunes, and the fiddlers were happy to oblige. People threw farthings, halfpennies, pennies into their offered hats. Someone even threw a silver sixpence in at one point; it may have been a mistake, but just in case, one of the fiddlers quickly stopped fiddling long enough to pocket the sixpence before anyone else did.

Yes, it was a merry night, and the crowd was in good cheer.

One woman, however, became slightly over-festive. It may have been the ale that went to her head. It may have been the heat. In any case, she was moved to give voice to her joy. She opened her wide mouth and started singing – and what a voice! All up and down the Grassmarket, shutters flew open as people leaned out to find the source of the racket.

'Heavens above, Jinty, would ye credit it? Somebody's killin a pig at this time o nicht!'

At first it was amusing; but try as they might, the fiddlers couldn't play loud enough to be heard above her. So the dancers began to lose step, and trip over each other in the dark. And the crowd wasn't ready to stop dancing. One of the innkeepers tried to hustle her away quietly, but the woman wasn't for being hustled. She belted him one on the lug, and just kept singing. So the constables were called, and then another two for reinforcements, and eventually four of them managed to drag this nuisance woman out of the way of the crowd, down the Cowgate and into the town jail for the night.

The duty clerk, peeved at having to work on such a night of festivities, was surly. He glared at the woman; he'd seen her many times before. But why should he make it easy for her?

'Name!' he barked.

'If ye dinna ken ma name by noo, Wullie Simpson, ye're no as smert as I aye thocht.'

'Mind yer manners wifie! What's yer name? I have tae write it doon in ma book.'

'Oh yer *book*, is it? My, you must be a right important bodie right enough if you have to write folks' names doon in a *book*.'

'Ye're no getting in without tellin me yer name.'

'Right then, ah'm no telling ye ma name.'

The woman looked around her, defiantly. Four constables stood behind her, looking bored but steadfast; there was no way they would let her escape. Wullie Simpson was giving her a headache; maybe she could do with a wee sleep after her long day of celebrations. There

would be a lot of clearing up to do later on; if she wasn't there, she couldn't be drawn into the chores. She decided to co-operate after all. Up to a point. She dropped him a curtsey, smiled sweetly with her toothless gums; 'It'll be Mistress Geddes to you,' she said, and stood by while the clerk wrote her name.

'Sign,' he ordered; and she took the pen and marked a large cross against her name, managing quite innocently to blot the whole page as she did so. Wullie Simpson tutted and grumbled and made her wait while he footered about with blotting paper. The he took a massive key which was dangling from a chain around his waist, unlocked an iron door, and creaked it open. The constables shoved her in – 'right Janey, behave yersel an ye'll get oot the morra,' and the door clanged shut behind her.

It was pitch dark. Janey ventured forward inch by inch and tripped over a bundle on the floor. A rat scurried over her foot and she screamed. The bundle on the floor woke up and cursed her loudly; and her long night in the cells began.

CHAPTER THREE

Peggy Murphy wasn't at all happy, having her peaceful sleep disturbed. She'd been in the middle of a lovely dream, back in the Mourne Mountains of Ireland. The hillsides were purple with heather, and in her dream she was a small child, maybe two or three years old, rattling along on a pony and trap with her mother, her father, her granny, and her older brother. Her mother dandled a new baby, her tiny sister, on her knee. It was a delicious dream. The fat little pony trotted along smartly, her father held her snugly round the shoulders, the baby cooed, and they all laughed as they bowled along. The sun shone warmly, the breeze was mild – all in all, it was a much nicer place to be than the cold damp cell she'd left behind in sleep.

'What in the devil's name is that?' she hissed into the dark.

'Lord Jesus help me!' cried Janey. 'Who's that?'

Peggy came to, and remembered, reluctantly, where she was. She peered into the dark but could see nothing. 'Is there anybody there?' she queried.

'Anither prisoner, nae worse than yersel,' replied

Janey with feeling, 'and there was no need to curse me. How was I to know you'd be lyin on the grund like a muckle sow?'

Peggy laughed. She'd often been called a muckle sow in daylight, when people could see her. She didn't mind; she quite liked sows. 'My name is Peggy Murphy. Pleased to meet ye. I hope we'll be good company for each other the night. And you would be...?'

'Janey Geddes. You're no fae roon these parts, are ye? I cannae place yer accent.'

'I'm pleased to meet you Janey. My home is in Ireland; I'm here for the harvest and then please God I'll be heading back home again to me own country.'

'Ireland! That's a long way away.'

'It is indeed. But we've been coming here every year since I was a small child. We help with liftin the tatties.'

'The tattie-howkin! I sometimes help wi the tattie-howkin masel. I'm pleased tae meet ye.' And she reached out to squeeze the woman's hand. Peggy and Janey fell to sharing their stories about the harvest, the places they had worked, the people they had met on the farms. It was inevitable that before long they would find a mutual acquaintance.

'Padraig Woods,' said Janey, 'I mind o him. A bonny fechter, a braw singer tae. He's fae Ireland an a. Dae ye ken him?'

'That's my cousin Padraig!' said Peggy. 'A fine man. Great at the howkin.'

Janey remembered something. 'But he was a catholic.'

'Aye?'

'You're no a catholic are ye?'

'I surely am. Maybe not as good a catholic as I should be, but a catholic nonetheless.'

Oh no!' cried Janey. 'As if it's no bad enough to be locked up in the cells a' night, I'm locked up wi a catholic!'

'And what's yer problem wi that now?'

'Never trust a catholic, that's what my mither always telt me.'

'Never trust a protestant, more like,' retorted Peggy. 'The troubles they cause. Rascals the lot o them. Burning down all them monasteries, the wanton destruction of it.'

'Only to get rid o a' the fause idols! It's youse lot that caused a' the bother at the reformation.'

'The reformation!' uttered Peggy with disdain, and Janey heard her spit on the floor. 'Wanton vandalism. All those fine churches burned to a cinder. What good did that do anyone, tell me?'

Janey and Peggy's dispute was interrupted at that point, as Wullie Simpson the clerk came rattling his key in the door. 'Will ye stop all that noise,' he cried, 'ye're disturbing the peace.' There was a bit of jostling at the door as he spoke to someone else. 'Just get in there and watch an no fa' ower onbody else, there's two women in there a'ready.' Then they heard hesitant footsteps, the clanging shut of the gate, the grating of the key in the lock, and the fast fading beat of Wullie Simpson's boots going back up the stairs.

'Who's that? What's yer name? Ower here, missus,' said Janey, trying to guide the woman through the darkness. There was no reply but a mutter, and they felt the woman groping to a place against the wall, and sitting down on a pile of straw.

13

Peggy joined in: 'have ye had a bad night my dear?' she queried.

'Bad enough,' was the short reply.

'My name's Janey Geddes and she's Peggy Murphy, fae Ireland, a catholic. What's your name? Where are ye fae?' Janey's curiosity was whetted.

'Just ca' me Bess.'

'Bess?' repeated Janey and Peggy together. 'Bess what?'

'Just Bess.'

'And where are ye fae, Bess?'

'Mind yer ain business.'

There was a shocked silence. Peggy and Janey were quite offended. They were just trying to make conversation. After all, in these circumstances, surely the woman should be glad of a bit of company?

'Never mind her,' said Peggy darkly, 'she'll be glad of a bit of crack before the night is over.'

'Must've ate a bad neep or somethin,' sniffed Janey. And they returned to their own discussions, but more mildly now, for they were united against the common enemy. Not that Bess was an enemy, but she clearly didn't want to be friends. Taking airs like that. It wasn't right.

CHAPTER FOUR

'Janey Geddes,' said Peggy thoughtfully. 'I'm sure I've heard your name before now.'

'You maybe heard tell of my mother,' said Janey. 'She was called Jenny – so am I really, but they called me Janey so as not to mix the two of us up. Jenny Geddes, she was. God rest her soul.'

'Aye that's it now! Jenny Geddes! Now remind me where I've heard of her before.'

Janey made herself comfortable. 'It's a long story,' she said, 'but I've the whole night to tell it, if you're interested.'

'I am that,' said Peggy, who loved a good story. '

Tell away.'

'It was a long, long time ago. I was just a lassie, about nine year auld. My mother kept a barra doon the Cowgate, sellin tatties an ingins an turnips an a' that.'

'I know that barrow! Is it still there? Is it the same one?' said Peggy, 'only me and my brother, that's where we stay when we're in Edinburgh, down one of the closes on the right hand side as you go down the brae. The barrow I'm thinking of, it's got a mended axle.'

'It is indeed, the very same. I mind when it cowped on the close an a' the tatties went rollin doon the gutter. That's when it got its axle mended. That barra's mine noo.'

'Your barrow!'

'Aye, it's me that sells the tatties an ingins these days.'

'Fancy that! Your own wee barrow!'

'Aye well, to get on wi ma story,' said Jenny, 'the auld King was still alive. Naebody roon aboot here liked him, no that we kent him, him an his fancy claes, an a' that hair. An the taxes! My pair mither paid oot a fortune in taxes, just to get the right to sell her ain tatties an ingins.

'Now you'll no likely agree wi this bit o the story, but I'll tell it anyway. Oor kirk in Scotland had sorted itsel oot, an we had oor ain wey o daein things. Plain an simple like. Just Jesus an the apostles, the Auld Testament an the Psalms. Nae Mary worshippin. Well here the auld king decided...'

'Let me interrupt you a wee minute,' said Peggy, 'what have you got against Our Lady?'

'Our Lady? Is that what you ca' her?'

'Indeed it is, the blessed mother of our Lord.'

'Nothin against her really, it's just that we dinna

\

16

worship her the way youse lot do.'

'Do ye not think people should honour their mothers?'

'Aye, I dae that.'

'So what are we arguing about?'

'Oh I dinnae ken, I just ken the catholics dae it a' fancy an we dae it plain. So – to get back to ma story...'

'Pardon me interruptin.'

'Right. Well, as I was sayin, the auld king was tryin to bring in a prayer book, just like what we had got rid o in the reformation!'

'Aye, the prayer book, what aboot it?'

'This bishop had wrote it, Bishop Rattray or some name like that. Anyway we didnae want prayer books, that's why we had the reformation. I think. Well maybe no just that, I cannae mind...

ST GILES

'Anyway, here this day, me an ma mither went up tae the kirk. Dae ye ken St. Giles, just up the road fae here?'

'I know it fine well. Just by the Heart of Midlothian.'

'Aye that's right. It wasna oor usual kirk, it was mair where the rich folk went, but for some reason that's where we went that day. I thocht a man came by the night before an gave her money to go to St. Giles that day, but I couldnae be sure. Maybe he was just payin his vegetable bill. But I thocht I saw silver coins. No much siller in vegetables. I didnae ask her what the siller was for, she didnae like us askin questions.'

'A man was giving her money? What would that be for?'

'Well I'm no sure aboot the man.'

'Maybe it was Oliver Cromwell!'

'Oliver Cromwell?'

Peggy spat on the ground. 'The devil himself, my father used to say. No friend to Ireland, that's for sure.'

'I dinna think it was Oliver Cromwell. Whit did Oliver Cromwell look like?

'Horns and cloven hoofs.'

'No, it wasna him. But anyway, as I was sayin... off we went to St. Giles in the mornin, her carryin her wee stool. That's what a' the women did, there was nae seats for them. They sat away at one side, on their wee stools. I didnae take a stool, I just sat on the flair along wi a the other weans. The men sat on the ither side, on the wooden pews. Well that's where the rich men sat. The poor men stood up at the back, no that many o them to be honest. My ain faither never went to the kirk except on special occasions. My mither was aye outspoken, an you could hear her a mile away – that's where I get my braw singin voice – an she used to say it was the women that kept the church goin. You can imagine what the men thocht o that for an idea.'

'Sure an me mother used to say the same thing.'

'Is that richt? Is it the same in your kirk?'

'I believe it's the same the world over.'

'Maybe you're richt. So. There we are, sittin in the kirk, waitin for the sermon to begin. Up gets the dean, an opens this prayer book, an tells us we're to read oot a these responses after he's said his bit!'

'What, like, the priest says *The Lord be with You*! and we say *And Also with You*?'

'Aye, just like that.'

'That's what we do,' said Peggy.

'Aye but we're no catholics, are we? We dinnae dae it like that. An the dean goes on, something aboot bein gathered here in Christ's name, an here before I know what's happenin, here's my mither on her feet! an shoutin oot at the dean!'

'Shouting out at the dean! What did she shout?'

'She shoutit, "daur ye speak the mass in ma lug?" an next thing, she's liftit up her stool and flung it as hard as she could, right at the dean's heid! Hit him right in the napper! An then she shouts, "De'il colic the wame o' ye!" An then all hell was let loose!'

'In the middle of the mass!'

'It wasnae the mass, it was the kirk!'

'Did they fling her out? Or was she put on your cutty stool?' Peggy was shocked and excited at such reckless behaviour.

'They couldnae catch her. Next thing you knew, everybody was heavin their stools at the pulpit. There was a crowd at the back that turned oot to be – wait till ye hear this - young apprentice laddies! They had dressed up as lassies wi cloaks and aprons, and come in the back wi their stools an a'; naebody noticed them at first. As soon as my mither threw the first stool, they a' joined in. Them as didnae have stools were flingin bibles. The dean was cooryin doon, tryin to hide under the communion table. It was a riot.'

Peggy couldn't believe her ears. 'Boys dressed as girls! Well fancy that now! And what happened next?'

'The constables were called, an they hauled away as mony as they could get hold o. But my mither an me escaped. We slid doon the back streets an were back hame by the time the constables came lookin for her, an they couldnae prove she'd been there.'

'So what happened to the prayer book?'

'Oh I dinnae ken. We never went back to St. Giles after that. I think they must have stopped usin it. Scots folk dinnae want a' that fuss in their worship.'

'Some of them do. I know some Scots catholics.'

'Aye well. Maybe the ones you know are a' right, I must say I've never had a conversation wi a catholic afore this night. You're no as odd as I'd have expected. I suppose ye're no daein any herm wi yer fancy weys if ye keep it tae yersels.'

'Well I'm much obliged to ye for your kind testimonial.'

'Dinna mention it.'

'Was the dean of St. Giles a catholic?'

'No, he was an Episcopalian.'

'What's that?'

'Some kind o funny in-the-middle thing.'

'What – neither one nor the tother?'

'Aye, I think so.'

'Strange.' Peggy was quiet for a moment. Then she asked, 'why would the apprentices stir up trouble, dressing up in girls' clothes and all that?'

'I dinnae ken. Maybe they got paid wi siller an a'. Maybe there was some rich folk that wantit a riot, but didnae want to get the blame o startin it.'

'All that carry on. And it's the same Jesus Mary and Joseph.'

'No it isnae... The very same? It cannae be. Are ye sure?'

'Sure as I'm sittin here. Now why do we have to fight each other, when the good Lord told us to live in peace?'

Janey said nothing. She had no answer. She couldn't think of a single reason to fight with Peggy over religion. But she knew that her own family and all her friends would be horrified at this – they thought that catholics were the work of the devil. She would have to keep her views to herself.

Both Janey and Peggy had forgotten all about Bess. But suddenly there was a piercing scream from Bess's direction, and Janey and Peggy nearly jumped out of their skins.

'What is it?' said Janey, jumping to her feet. But Peggy knew what it was; she'd heard that same scream many times before. She felt her way over, on her hands and knees, to where Bess was sitting up against the cell wall, sweating and moaning.

'It's all right lass,' she said to Bess. 'We'll see to you.'

'What is it?' cried Janey.

Peggy paused. 'Have you ever helped deliver a baby before?'

'A baby? No, I havena...'

'Well that's a pity; but better late than never. Give me your cloak. We're working in the dark here. Just do as I tell you and we'll be all right.'

'Have you ever done this before?'

'Many, many times.' And Peggy turned to Bess.

'Now don't fret my dear. Just do as I tell you. Janey and I will make sure you and your baby are all right.' And Janey heard her add, under her breath, 'please God and Our Lady.'

Silently, Janey handed her cloak over to Peggy, and stood by to take instructions. It was still pitch dark. This was the scariest thing that had ever happened to her. Somehow through the years she had managed to avoid babies and their horrors. If that cell gate hadn't been firmly locked, she'd have been out of there, and no mistake.

As for Bess – she had no choice but let nature take its course, assisted by two blethering strangers whom she'd met in the least promising of circumstances. One of them completely useless, the other one claiming to know what she was doing - but it could all just be Irish blarney as far as Bess knew. Not perhaps the best place to be in for bringing your first and dearest into the world. Bess cursed herself for her stupidity in getting into this hopeless situation.

But there was nothing else for it. She was just going to have to do as the Peggy woman told her. And hope for the best.

CHAPTER FIVE

Peggy was a skilled midwife but she had never had to deliver a baby in the pitch dark before. She told Janey to shout for Wullie Simpson, and Janey, with a voice like a bull in a thicket, shouted at the top of her lungs for Wullie Simpson to come - but to no avail. Even if he'd let them have a candle, it would have helped. And maybe an extra blanket. But no - either he'd deserted his post, or he just didn't want to be disturbed. So between them, Peggy and Janey gathered what straw they could, and managed to get

Bess into a relatively comfortable position. Then Peggy took control.

Janey was secretly glad it was dark; she didn't like this turn off events at all. But what else could they do? Bess's baby was ready to be born, it seemed, and it wasn't going to wait for the convenience of daylight, hot water, blankets, or brandy.

'This isn't your first baby is it, lass?' asked Peggy; and bit her lip in fear as Bess told her that it was indeed her first. It would have helped if Bess had known what to expect; but she didn't. When Janey said she was new to birthing too, and didn't think she'd be much help, that was the last straw. As if there was a choice! 'Well you'll just have to learn fast,' she snapped. 'We're all in this together and I need help here. So pay attention.'

Poor Bess was in terrible pain, and Peggy told her just to scream as loud as she wanted – it wasn't as if they had to worry about waking up the neighbours; in fact it would be a help if she could. So Bess screamed and pushed, Peggy uttered instructions, and Janey, terrified, for once in her life did exactly as she was told. This mainly involved mopping Bess's brow and rubbing her back, and shouting in vain for Wullie Simpson.

Childbirth was often dangerous in those days. It wasn't at all uncommon for mothers to die in the process. Babies, too, were often stillborn. And you never knew if the baby would be all right. Peggy had supervised hundreds of births, and perhaps only half of them had gone completely smoothly. She knew that even in the best of conditions, even rich ladies in fine feather beds with doctors in attendance, the risks were high. Secretly, in her heart, she feared the worst, and my! would she make trouble for the authorities and Wullie Simpson if either Bess or her baby died tonight.

'Say your prayers, Janey,' she told her assistant, and began her own: 'Holy Mary, Mother of God...'

Janey's heart was hammering. Even though she had never been involved in birthing, and never had a baby herself, she knew it was a risky business. 'What will I pray for?' she asked.

'God's grace.'

The three women laboured on. It seemed to Janey that it took an awful long time. There would be ten minutes of screaming and pushing followed by half an hour of panting and resting. Every time it seemed as if the baby must come this time, the moment would pass. But the panting and resting sessions became shorter and shorter, and eventually Peggy's voice rose in excitement: 'This is it, Bess! Good girl! Push hard now! The baby's coming!'

And all of a sudden, it was over. Bess gave an almighty scream and Peggy had a tiny new baby in her hands. Quickly she used her petticoat to wipe its nose and mouth and eyes, wrapped it up in Janey's shawl, and as it started to cry, passed it to the exhausted and anxious Bess. 'Here you are Bess, it's a wee boy. He needs a feed. Well done the pair of you. Thank the Lord for a safe delivery.'

'A safe delivery? Thank the Lord he put *you* in this cell tonight,' said Bess, and started sobbing as she clasped the new baby and held him to her breast.

'Shhh, now, shhh, everything's fine.'

As the first grey streaks of daylight came filtering down from the small, dirty window high up in the cell wall, the three women examined the baby boy for defects. And there were none. He was perfect in every respect.

'I'm that grateful to you Peggy. And to you, Janey. I'm sorry I was rude to youse earlier on. I was just worried. It could all have gone so wrong...'

'Shhhh, Bess, this is a night none of us'll forget in a hurry. You get some sleep now that you've fed him. He'll be needing a wee sleep as well after all his hard work. We'll watch him for you.'

And Bess drifted off into a deep, deep sleep while Janey held the baby and Peggy cleared up the mess as best she could. The women couldn't believe it had all gone so well. It was a miracle. This baby, they both privately thought, must be meant for great things.

Tiredness caught up with them; and they had all drifted off to a deep sleep by the time Wullie Simpson came stamping down the stairs to tell them it was time to get away home.

CHAPTER SIX

Wullie had managed to join the celebrations after he'd gone off shift last night. The bonfire in the Grassmarket had been kept well stoked up, there was still plenty good meat on the hog roast, and the ale was flowing ever more freely. Soon he had forgotten his irritation at having to work on the most historic night of the year, as he caught up with the news, gobbled down some meat and ale, and relaxed into the festivities. The fiddlers fiddled on, the jigs and reels having given way to the slower, gentler ballads and gavottes. All up and down the street, people sat around in groups, singing along to the scrape of the strings. Rich and poor, men and women, all were joined in harmony after the best feast they'd seen in years. This, they hoped, was a sign of good things to come. Peace reigned. Strangers embraced, old enemies forgave each other, and friends blessed foes. What did all the old political and religious differences matter, they asked themselves? What was important was enough food and drink in your belly, a roof over your head at night, and someone to love. A new king was on the throne, God was in his heaven and all was right with the world.

It was about four in the morning before Wullie Simpson got home to his own bed, and he wasn't anywhere near ready to get up when the seven o'clock handbell sounded in the street above his head, clattered back and forth by a young boy in rags. So he rolled over and went back to sleep. An hour later the eight o'clock handbell sounded, and he staggered out of his cot in search of a drink of water. Nobody, he thought, would care about him being late back to work on an occasion like this. On the other hand, once he had clerked out his prisoners, he'd be able to come straight back home to bed. 'Might as well go and get it over with,' he thought. 'Or will I leave them to stew for another hour or so?' Then he remembered Janey Geddes singing, and hurriedly jumped into his stockings and shoes and made for the town jail.

He wasn't looking for complications. So he was outraged to find that in a cell where he had clerked in three people the night before, there were now four to be clerked out. 'There must be some procedure for this,' he growled, 'how am I to explain this to the Chief Magistrate?' And he

went off to see if anybody knew how to do the paperwork
for an extra body that had materialised out of thin air.

The Assitant Chief Magistrate was bemused. 'What
do you mean, an extra body? Are you telling me someone
broke *in* to prison during the night? Usually they're trying
to break out!'

'It's a baby.'

'A baby? How did that get there?'

'By the usual manner I believe, sir.'

The Assistant Chief Magistrate coughed. He didn't

want to hear the details; he knew that Wullie Simpson wouldn't want to give him them. This was women's business. All that messy stuff. But still you had to get the paperwork more or less right. In case the woman forgot to register the birth with the parish, as no doubt she would.

'Just take its name and details down. If anyone asks any questions, I'll explain.'

So Wullie Simpson stamped back down to the cells where Janey and Peggy and Bess were growing increasingly impatient to be let out. They were hungry; they wanted food and drink and a wash, and a comfortable bed to catch up on their sleep. Bess wanted to find her mother or, failing that, her aunt, and explain about the boy, and hopefully get some looking after. None of them wanted to be hanging about a cold and dirty prison cell while Wullie Simpson fussed and footered about with paperwork. So they gave him some abuse when he arrived back down the stone steps.

'About time! Get us out o here, you've no right keeping us waiting all this time!'

'Auld Simpson's oot o his depth, he doesnae ken whit tae dae wi a new bairn!'

'Come on, come on, it's cauld doon here and my bairn's needin fed.'

'Feed it then, I'm not stopping you,' said Wullie, and busied himself with the big clerking-in book while Bess adjusted her clothing to feed the hungry baby. 'Right then ladies,' he said, 'Janey Geddes, you are cautioned to be of good behaviour and to appear in court tomorrow morning, today being Sunday, for sentencing. Sign here.' Janey took the quill and scrawled the messiest cross she could manage. Janey stood to the side.

'Peggy Murphy, you are cautioned to be of good behaviour and to appear in court tomorrow morning, today being Sunday, for sentencing. Sign here.' Peggy took the quill and marked a neat cross next to her name. Then she stood aside by the open gate, waiting for Bess to be clerked out.

'Bess known as Forsyth, you are cautioned to be of good behaviour and to appear in court tomorrow morning, today being Sunday, for sentencing. Sign here.' Bess took the quill and marked her cross. She made to leave.

'Wait!' Wullie stretched his arm across the cell door. He pointed to the baby. 'Name?'

Bess stared at Wullie. 'He hasna got a name yet.'

'Well you'd better give him one. He canna leave

without a name.'

Janey and Peggy tutted and muttered; 'De'il colic ye,' said Janey, 'let the lassie be.'

Peggy looked at Bess. 'Have you got a name for him, dearie? His father's name, maybe?'

Bess looked scornful at this suggestion. 'I dinna ken. Let me think.' She looked at the baby. 'Does he look like a wee John? or a Thomas? or a Davie?' The baby slept innocently. None of these names seemed to fit him.

'He's going to be a strong wee laddie that one,' said Peggy, 'after what he went through last night. 'He'll grow to be a great man.'

Wullie was getting impatient. He wanted back to his bed. 'Will you just get a move on and give it a name,' he growled.

'He's no an It, he's a he,' said Bess, and looked again at the baby. 'I know. I'll call him Charles, for the new king!' and the baby grunted contentedly in his sleep.

That's it!' cried Janey and Peggy, 'he knows his name already!'

Bess looked at Wullie. 'His name is Charles Geddes Murphy Forsyth'. Janey and Peggy were delighted, and Wullie slowly and painstakingly wrote the name down in his ledger: 'Charles..... Geddes...... Murphy...... Forsyth. There.'

Bess moved to pass him onto the stairs, but again Wullie put his hand across the cell door. 'Religion?'

'What? Religion! You never asked us our religion!'

'Ah but this is different.

'How is it different?'

'Ladies,' threatened Wullie, 'I could just lock you back up again and that would solve the problem. Now.

Religion?'

'None,' said Bess.

'You have to have a religion. Catholic or Protestant?' said Wullie

Bess looked as if she was ready to murder Wullie Simpson. 'It disnae matter!' she protested.

'I think you'll find it does, Mistress Forsyth.'

Janey and Peggy had had enough. 'Would you listen to me now,' said Peggy, 'I've brought many bairns into this world and they all need their God, but this bairn doesn't need to be the one or the tother if his mother doesn't want him to be. His mother knows best what's good for him.'

'That's all very well, but...' began Wullie.

'Listen Mister,' put in Janey, 'if you ever get to spend a night in the cells, you'll ken fine it doesnae matter a whit, whether you're a catholic or a protestant. And I never thought I would hear mysel sayin that.'

Wullie wasn't going to budge on this one. He knew all too well how important matters of religion were to his masters. He put down his quill and crossed his arms. 'Catholic or Protestant?' he repeated.

Janey, Peggy and Bess looked at each other. Men! They came to a decision, nodded to each other, and went into action. Peggy and Janey grabbed Wullie by the oxters and heaved him out of the way of the door. Bess made good her escape, running as fast as she could up the stone steps and out into the pale morning sunshine which filtered down through the high tenements into Edinburgh's Royal Mile. She clasped young Charles Geddes Murphy Forsyth to her bosom. 'Look, son,' she whispered, holding him up to the light, 'this is your toon; this is Edinburgh!'

Janey and Peggy held onto Wullie Simpson, his legs

waggling about above the ground, for a good two minutes.
Then they shoved him into the cell, clanged the door shut
behind him, and legged it up the steps. Of course Wullie
had the keys, he'd be right out behind them; but they had
a good start on him. By the time they reached street level,
there was no sign of Bess or young Charles.

They said a hurried goodbye; they could hear Wullie
Simpson gasping up the stairs behind them.
'Peggy – I'll no forget this nicht. God bless ye. Ye've
taught me somethin I'll never forget.''
Janey – mind me in yer prayers and I'll mind ye in mine.
And pray for wee Charlie Forsyth.'
Wullie Simpson came gasping out of the close mouth
behind them, and they scarpered, Janey up the street and
Peggy down. Wullie ran round in circles for a few seconds,
unable to decide which one to follow; then gave up and
with a bad grace went back down the stone steps to sort

his ledger.

The following morning in court, when the names of Janey Geddes, Peggy Murphy and Bess Forsyth were called out, none of them appeared. Warrants were issued for their arrest. More paperwork was issued.

Back in their own, very different lives, each of the three women knew that God would look after them, and also after the baby boy born in such squalid circumstances. They all followed their own ways of worshipping; and each night before they went to sleep, though far apart, they never forgot to pray for the same thing:

'Lord God look after Charles Geddes Murphy Forsyth and keep him in your ways; and let it never matter whether he is a catholic or a protestant. Amen.'

GLOSSARY

CRACK Conversation

INGINS Onions

LUG Ear (as in 'she belted him one on the lug' – meaning that she hit him on the ear, or the side of his head; or 'daur ye speak the mass in ma lug?' – meaning that this was something she didn't want to hear)

NAPPER Head

OXTERS Armpits

NEEP Turnip

SILLER Silver, or meaning 'money'

SOW A female pig

WAME Womb, or stomach (as in 'De'il colic the wame o' ye' – meaning 'may the devil give you colic')

READERS' NOTES

Monarchy and Religion: Until 1603, when Queen Elizabeth I of England died, England and Scotland had separate thrones. But Elizabeth had no children, and James VI of Scotland was appointed as her successor, and became James I of England.

By that time, Scotland was a Protestant country, although there were continuing troubles over religion. In England, James was head of the Church of England, which struck a middle line between the roman catholic faith, and the extremes of the reformed church. James used his new position as king of both countries to extend the English approach to religion in Scotland. Between 1604 and 1612 he instituted bishops; and the merchants, especially in Edinburgh, were taxed heavily to pay for this.

James died in 1625 and his son, Charles I, came to the throne. Although he had been born in Scotland, Charles rarely came here, and knew very little of Scottish customs and preferences. He outraged people by imposing English styles of worship, including the introduction of an Anglican prayer book in 1637.

On Sunday, July 23rd 1637, a riot erupted in St. Giles Cathedral when the Dean began reading from the new prayer book. It is said that Jenny Geddes cried traitor, and hurled her stool at the dean.

Jenny's existence is not well chronicled in history, and this author finds it difficult to understand how a mere woman (women being very low in influence at that time) could have led the rebellion single-handed. There are some theories that she was encouraged by others, more powerful than herself, to front the riot; nevertheless there is a plaque today in St. Giles Cathedral which says that Jenny struck a blow for Scottish freedom of worship.

The English didn't like Charles I and in 1649 they beheaded him. A period of republicanism followed, with Oliver Cromwell as a military leader who led severe reprisals against the Catholics. Meantime the Scots hadn't approved the beheading of Charles I, and proclaimed as king his son, Charles II, in defiance of England. Charles II was crowned at Scone Palace in 1650; but Scotland was deeply divided and came under military rule from England. Charles was eventually obliged to flee abroad until 1660 when the monarchy was restored across Great Britain. This story, 'Reformed! A story of Jenny Geddes' is set at the celebrations for the restoration of Charles I to the throne across Britain.

Throughout this time, religion was a vital force in people's lives and was seen as a legitimate and important cause of war.

Money: in old currency, a **guinea** was a pound and a shilling. There were twenty shillings in a pound; so one guinea was 21 shillings; two guineas were two pounds and two shillings or 42 shillings; and so on. Further to this, there were twelve pennies in a shilling; a **farthing** was a quarter of a penny and a **halfpenny** – well, you can guess. If you paid five pounds, fourteen shillings and threepence halfpenny for something (say, a cow), the sum of money would be written down like this:

£5/14/3 ½d

British currency was known as LSD – L for pounds, S for shillings, and D for pence. Not exactly straightforward. However it remained like this until 1971 when the British money system was decimalised.

Paperwork: Wullie Simpson's preoccupation with getting the records right seems utterly trivial. However in those days, when very few people could read and write, the recording of daily events was recognised as important. Historians nowadays rely heavily on records like these to understand the past. When people couldn't read or write, they marked an X against their name as a signature.

The church and punishment: Peggy refers to the 'cutty stool' in her discussions with Jane. In those days, the church was given responsibility for ensuring people's good behaviour, and those who didn't behave would be forced to sit on a stool at the front of the church during the service. Abuse would be hurled, and generally it was a humiliating experience, and one which people would not be anxious to repeat.

Dean: the dean was the head minister in a cathedral; the 'heid bummer'.

Immigration: Throughout the centuries, people have moved around from country to country in search of better living conditions. There have always been many Irish in Scotland (and vice versa); even in the 17th century, people came over during the harvest

Teachers reading this may wish to note that this book dovetails with the Scottish curriculum in

- Environmental Studies
- Personal and Social Health Education
- Philosophy
- Language

Further information on Rooshie-Doo books, and suggestions for their use in schools, can be found on the publisher's website at www.galluspublications.com

If you have enjoyed this book, you may also enjoy…

Cannibals! A story of Sawney Bean by Helen Welsh

Murderers! A story of Burke and Hare by Karen Doherty

Threat! A story of Mary Slessor by Karen Doherty

Accused! A story of Beatrix Laing by Susan Greig